MW01036381

Business Leaders Are Raving About The Priority Promise

"This is a must share book for friends and business associates as a staple for business training and a must-have guide when success seems to engulf life."

Darryl Baskin, CEO and Owner
The Baskin Real Estate Specialists

"The Priority Promise has simplified the process that all of us need to implement in order to optimize our relationships, business effectiveness, and personal joy. As the seasons of our lives change, we need to make other changes that will likely only occur if we have a systematic way to think about them. Implementing his system now will allow each of us to enjoy the benefits of a new life-long habit."

Phil Smith, Author
A Billion Bootstraps

"From the time I was little, I can always remember my mother telling me that "the key to a happy, healthy life was BALANCE." Finally, someone tells us how to really achieve balance in a step by step, process. The Priority Promise provides the best practical, "how-to" advice, I have ever read."

Julie Hakman, President and CEO
American Checked

"As I read The Priority Promise, I couldn't wait to get through all the steps. A close friend of mine has been trying to overcome so many of the same things this describes. He has been re-reading self-help books but to no avail. Sean, you may have just provided him with the answer! Thank you!"

Gina Wilson , President and CEO
Oklahoma Central Credit Union

"I just finished reading The Priority Promise and immediately found myself evaluating my own life with your key principles. I will use the book's principles to more effectively set priorities and stop letting lesser things rank equally with the things I really want to do and achieve."

Tom Wenrick, Owner
Wenrick Development

"I very much believe in the concept and method that The Priority Promise identifies. The Parable of The Talents has convinced me that I need to identify the skills that God has blessed me with and place a greater priority related to those involvements."

James Brock, Owner
Brock and Associates

"The Priority Promise is outstanding. It is simple and to the point. I have never thought of life as one bucket priority. This is a much more effective plan than compartmentalizing our career versus our personal life."

Steve Dobbs, CEO
Urologic Specialists of Oklahoma

"I just read The Priority Promise, and it rang right home to me. I only wish I could have gone through a process like this when I was in my thirties or forties."

Marvin Morse, CEO and Owner
Morse & Associates, CPA

"The Priority Promise has dished up something that I can get my arms around in the midst of all of the self-improvement and personal organizational noise that fills the bookshelves."

Kevin Jordan, CEO and Owner
Black Gold Group

"The Priority Promise is a wonderful plan for anybody struggling to keep their priorities straight and accomplish everything they want in life."

J.J. Hurley, CEO and Owner
GDH Consulting, Inc.

THE PRIORITY PROMISE

7 STEPS TO START OWNING YOUR LIFE AND LIVING YOUR PRIORITIES

This book is dedicated to Grandma Charlotte.

Your life serves as an example to us all.

The Priority Promise
ISBN: 978-0-9889281-1-4
Copyright © 2013 by Sean Kouplen

Published by
Yorkshire Publishing
6271 E. 120th Court
Suite 200
Tulsa, OK 74137
www.yorkshirepublishing.com

Text Design: Lisa Simpson
www.SimpsonProductions.net

TABLE OF CONTENTS

FOREWORD

Sean Kouplen was a close friend of mine before we began our coaching relationship. I knew that no one had a bigger heart or wanted to do more for others than Sean, but he was frustrated and overwhelmed. He felt like he was spread too thin and just wasn't doing a good job at anything. Haven't we all felt this way at some point in our lives?

Sean, like many of us, didn't just need a new time management system. This wouldn't be enough. He needed a paradigm shift, a new way to manage his life. I shared some ideas with Sean that had a profound impact on him and his relationships with others.

Immediately, he changed. He felt (and looked) less stressed and hurried. His conversations with others became deeper, his relationships began to flourish, and he began to enjoy life again.

He was so excited about his experience that he began to organize these ideas and shared them with other executives. The results were so amazing that he decided to share his experience with others. He created a process called The Priority Promise Life Management System, and it has been used by people from all walks of life with great success.

I believe you will see a huge change in your life if you practice The Priority Promise system. We all want to live an abundant life filled with joy and deep, meaningful relationships. This is your first step in making it happen.

Dr. Steve Greene, Dean
Oral Roberts University College of Business

PREFACE

Why should you implement the seven-step Priority Promise Life Management System? Quite simply, the alternative isn't very attractive.

Navigating today's busy world without some type of life management system is virtually impossible. How many people do you know that excel in one area of their life, only to completely fail in another area?

In the banking business, I deal with individuals who are extremely successful on a professional level. They have great business acumen and put all their energy and time into growing their net worth and building their corporate empire.

They often fail, however, in managing their other roles. They find their marriages struggling, their relationships with their children nonexistent, they have failed to take care of themselves and they have few close personal relationships. They focus their time and effort in one role (or a few closely related roles) with no plan or discipline to manage the other important areas of their life.

The Priority Promise system literally changed my life. I wrote this book because I believe it can change your life too. We must all learn to prioritize our lives in such a way that the important roles are satisfied first and we are realistic about what we can accomplish within our available time.

Please enjoy the book and I sincerely hope that *The Priority Promise* has a profound impact on your life.

Sean Kouplen, Author
The Priority Promise

1

MR. SUCCESSFUL

I don't know the key to success, but the key to failure is trying to please everybody.
—*Bill Cosby*

Has your life ever felt out of control?

At the age of 39, I was blessed beyond my wildest dreams. I had a great marriage, three beautiful children, served as the CEO of a growing community bank, and was a business owner, a church elder, a successful author and speaker, and a community leader.

I had received every award you can imagine, including being named Citizen of the Year for my hometown, top alumni for my fraternity, outstanding adjunct professor for my university, and one of Oklahoma's Most Admired CEOs. By all indications, I appeared to have it made.

The truth, however, was that my life always felt out of control. I was constantly behind and could never seem to catch up.

My days were completely reactive as I focused on the urgent problems of the day and never on causes or relationships that were the most important to me. Weeks and months would fly by with little time to enjoy life. I had this nagging fear that my life was slipping away while I tackled my unmanageable to-do list.

I was most concerned that I never seemed to be "present." When others would talk to me, I would think about something else. I was always mentally determining what I needed to do next. I felt a constant pressure to perform and didn't want to let others down—my family, my employees, or my shareholders.

I tried to work harder, but that didn't work. I got up earlier and stayed up later, but that didn't work. I tried every time management technique on the planet, and they didn't work either.

I didn't need another time management tip—I needed a paradigm shift. It was time for real, lasting change.

2

THE INVISIBLE GRANDSON

Life is what happens when you are busy making other plans.
—John Lennon

It was a chilly fall afternoon as I hurriedly drove down Memorial Drive in Tulsa, Oklahoma, from one meeting (which went longer than planned) to another. My thoughts suddenly turned to my Grandma Charlotte.

I needed to call Grandma Charlotte—I missed her. She was eighty-three years old, but acted like she was fifty. She was cute, cool, and trendy. We loved to talk about business and politics. We shared a very special bond.

I hadn't seen her since our family's Fourth of July party. My sister told me that at recent family events, Grandma called me "the invisible grandson" and this really bothered me.

It wasn't that I didn't love or think about Grandma. I thought about her daily. I wondered how she was feeling and longed to talk to her. I knew she was getting older, and I wanted to cherish time with her while I could.

The problem was that I just never seemed to have time. During the day, I was booked to the minute. At night and on the weekends, I was being a husband and a dad. Early in the morning, when I had some time for myself, it was too early to call.

So, as I drove down Memorial, I looked at my watch. I had about ten minutes before my next meeting. I picked up my iPhone and got ready to call Grandma Charlotte. Then I noticed that I had three urgent emails from the office that I needed to handle. Instead of calling Grandma Charlotte, I answered the emails.

This was the cycle of thinking that always kept me from calling or visiting my precious Grandma Charlotte. Day after day, week after week, month after month, I let other things get in the way.

3

REALITY CHECK

Face reality as it is, not as it was or as you wish it to be.
—Jack Welch

I am a pleaser by nature. I want to make people happy and proud of me. Knowing that Grandma called me the invisible grandson broke my heart. I never wanted her to feel like she wasn't a priority to me. I didn't want to let her down.

My concern wasn't only about Grandma Charlotte. It was about my life in general. Many relationships had been placed on the back burner, including those with my sister, my parents, my best friends from high school and college, and friends from church. I never had the time to reach out to these people. I knew relationships were important, but I couldn't seem to squeeze them into my busy life.

My life seemed to be one big blur. I was getting up early and working late, running from meeting to meeting, always ten to twenty phone calls and fifty to sixty emails behind. The harder I worked, the more I fell behind. My to-do list kept getting longer and longer with very little improvement. I knew I needed to take time for myself to exercise, read, and relax, but I rarely did these things. I would occasionally take clients out to play golf or take a short trip with my buddies, but I even felt stressed and guilty during these times.

I tried everything. I prioritized my tasks and classified my to-do list into various categories. I delegated. I segmented my time and grouped similar tasks together. I worked very hard and was efficient by any definition of the word, but it wasn't helping. I couldn't keep up.

That night as I drove home from work, I finally took the time to call Grandma Charlotte. As we talked, she told me that everyone's life just seemed to get busier and busier. No one had time to talk or enjoy life anymore. She felt like our world was spinning out of control and she was worried about me because I was spread so thin.

I was worried about me too.

4

THE FIRST STEP

Effective leadership is putting first things first. Effective management is discipline in carrying it out.
—Stephen Covey

D r. Steve Greene had been a good friend of mine for almost 10 years. Steve was the dean of the Oral Roberts University (ORU) College of Business and the pastor of Bixby Community Church, where we served as elders together. Steve served on multiple nonprofit boards, including being chairman of our local Chamber of Commerce, taught multiple classes, and gave marketing presentations on a regular basis.

Steve was tremendously busy, but he always seemed prepared and engaged. His church sermons alone must have taken ten hours or more to develop, and they were always of the highest quality.

Steve cared about people. He always seemed to keep his commitments, and he performed tasks and duties with great care. He always had time to talk when I called, and I know that he spent many hours in counseling sessions with those who needed it. He was thoughtful and would call me to check on important dates or times in my life. How did he do it?

I called Steve to share my frustration with my poor time management skills and ask for his advice. I thought maybe he could give me some ideas for improving in these areas.

"Steve," I told him, "they always say that the first step of any effective recovery program is admitting that you need help, and I certainly need help!"

He laughed and said he knew exactly how I felt. "Sean, it is very normal for someone your age and with your responsibilities to struggle with managing their life. I certainly struggled when I was your age, but I had a mentor who taught me a few strategies that made a huge impact on my life."

"Steve, could you teach me these strategies?"

Steve said he would do his best to help me, but I would need to make this a top priority. He said that the strategies were very involved and, in his experience, the process worked better if the strategies were implemented one at a time over a period of several weeks.

At that point in time, I would have done anything to get my life under control. We agreed on a regular meeting time and place.

Steve and I met every week for ninety minutes, although I struggled to set aside the time. An hour and a half seems like an eternity when you are constantly behind.

I spent the first couple of meetings sharing my frustrations and challenges. Steve asked great questions and seemed to understand my situation. At the end of our second meeting, Steve announced that he was ready to start sharing his life management strategies.

5

ROLE MANAGEMENT

"When I am sixty, I should be attempting to achieve different personal goals than those which had priority at age twenty."
—*Warren Buffett*

A week passed before my third meeting with Steve. That week confirmed my need for a drastic change.

Every day was filled with back-to-back meetings. I enjoyed meeting new people, landing new clients for the bank, and giving business advice, but the work was stacking up while I was in meetings.

Incoming phone calls and emails were piling up, important projects were behind schedule, and my best clients were complaining that I wasn't as accessible as I used to be.

I had no time to manage, think, or plan. I worked late every night and got up early the next morning to do it all over again. My conversations with clients or employees were brief and superficial because I was always running late or thinking about my growing to-do list.

When I got home, I was so exhausted that I didn't feel like playing with my kids or talking to my wife. On top of all of this, I had this nagging feeling that I should call certain friends and family members to see how they were doing, but I just didn't have the time or energy.

On Thursday afternoon at 3:30 p.m., I walked into our weekly meeting full of anticipation. Dr. Greene was early, as usual, while I was ten minutes late.

"These life management strategies are going to take us several weeks," he said. "Before we begin implementing our strategies, I need for you to commit to completing the homework every week. No excuses, okay?" He knew how crazy my life was and my propensity for overcommitment. I agreed.

I wanted to live again, to enjoy life. I wanted to deepen my relationships with others and invest in friendships that I had neglected for too long. I wanted to be present and not feel stressed and behind every second of the day.

Steve began explaining the strategies to me.

"Sean, my mentor taught me that our lives are really made up of a series of roles. Some roles are more important than others and our success in life is determined by how well we perform in our most important roles.

"My goal is to help you develop a process that will allow you to prioritize your roles, allocate adequate time for each, and hold yourself accountable for continuous improvement in each of your most critical roles. Let's begin by defining all of your roles," he said. "Who is Sean Kouplen?"

"Can you help me understand exactly what you mean by roles?" I asked.

"We all play different roles throughout our lives. I am a pastor, husband, father, grandfather, college professor, manager, fundraiser, golfer, nonprofit board chairman, business advisor, etc. We need to list all of the roles you play in your life."

What an interesting way of looking at life. I had never thought of my life as a series of roles before.

"I understand, Steve. I have many roles, maybe too many. They include husband, father, son, grandson, brother, friend, Sunday school teacher, church elder, Regent Bank CEO and board member, business owner, member of several nonprofit boards, member of two corporate boards, author, and speaker."

"Wow, you do have a lot of roles," Steve laughed, "but I think you are still missing some. Certain major roles, such as CEO, actually have several roles within them. We need to discuss your different roles within that position."

"What do you mean Steve?"

"What are the various responsibilities you have as CEO?"

"As CEO, I have several responsibilities. I am the strategist and visionary for our company. I manage, and hopefully motivate, our employees. I develop new relationships and new business for the bank. I communicate regularly with our investors to make sure they know they are important to our organization, and I oversee our advertising and marketing efforts."

"Now you are getting it!" Steve exclaimed! "CEO includes multiple roles such as strategist, manager, business developer and investor relations. This week I want you to think about *all* of the roles in your life and make a comprehensive list."

"Before you start, let me give you two final tips. First, be sure to include a role for self-improvement such as exercise, reading, and self-reflection. We all need to invest in ourselves.

Early in my life, self-improvement activities such as consistent exercise, reading, spiritual development, and personal reflection didn't seem to be critical. As I have grown older, they have become very important.

The self-improvement role has proven to be the glue that holds my life together. Exercise, reading, spiritual development, and personal reflection give me energy and a more healthy perspective. They are very important to my ongoing happiness and productivity."

"That makes perfect sense, Steve. What is your second tip?"

"Second, be sure to also include any roles that you wish you were playing, but might not be playing right now."

"Roles I wish I was playing?"

"Yes. Let's assume you have always wanted to be an author, but you weren't taking the time to start writing. You should add this to your role list. Or, let's say you wanted to start a new hobby. Add this to your list."

Steve continued. "Sean, please take your time when defining your roles. This is a critical stage within the Priority Promise life management system. One of our biggest mistakes is that we become so busy that we forget certain roles within our lives. Rediscovering those roles can be a life-changing process for you."

I spent every night of the next week brainstorming about my roles. I dissected my life into four quadrants: family, business, extracurricular/community, and personal.

My family roles included husband, father, brother, son, and grandson.

My business roles included supervisor, visionary/strategist, business developer, client relations and service, marketing director, business advisor, and investor relations.

My extracurricular/community roles included various board positions for various nonprofit and community organizations.

My personal roles included friend, author, speaker, ongoing self-improvement efforts such as reading, exercise, and spiritual development, and recreational time.

I found that certain roles dominated my life while I allowed others to be completely neglected. No wonder I felt so stretched and disconnected all the time!

When all was said and done, I ended up with a lengthy list of roles that I currently practiced or wanted to practice.

I was beginning to understand why my life always felt so unmanageable.

STEP 1:

⚜

Make a list of the roles within your life.

Include all existing roles, new roles you want to start playing, and roles for self development and improvement.

6

THE BIG ROCKS

Most of us spend too much time on what is urgent and not enough time on what is important.
                                                        —*Stephen R. Covey*

S teve thought my role list looked great.

"This is a fantastic start," he said. "I can definitely see why you are having some time management challenges, but now it's really going to get interesting. Have you ever seen the big rock demonstration?"

"No, I don't think so."

"The big rock demonstration is a visual way to think of time management and prioritization. You start with a jar and lots of rocks of different sizes. If you put the small gravel rocks in first, there isn't room for the big rocks. But, if you put the big rocks in first, the small rocks will then fill all around them."

"The big rocks are our most important tasks or roles while the little rocks are less important. If we allow the small rocks, or less important tasks, to take over our time, there's no room for the important things."

"Sean, the next step is for you to prioritize your roles from most important to least important. Which roles are your big rocks and which roles are your smaller rocks? This can be a little overwhelming, so I suggest you break them into three categories."

"'A' priorities are those that are critical to your ongoing happiness and success. If you do not succeed in these roles, your life will be drastically impacted.

"'B' priorities are important, but not quite as critical as 'A' priorities. You have a strong desire to succeed in these roles, but the consequences won't be catastrophic if you don't.

"'C' priorities are those that you could do without if you had to. You enjoy them and there is clearly a reason that you have these roles, but they could be discontinued with minimal consequences."

Steve continued. "When determining your most important roles, keep in mind that we all have certain gifts and passions. Your top priorities should be consistent with these gifts and passions."

This assignment was tough. I am a pleaser and never want to let anyone down, so it was very difficult for me to list certain roles low on the list. After several days of prioritizing and re-prioritizing my roles, I finalized my list.

I found that certain 'A' roles such as husband, father, manager, and business developer were critical to success and fulfillment in my life. If I did not perform well in those roles, my life could change drastically for the worse.

I also found that certain self-development roles, such as exercise, reading, and personal reflection, didn't seem as critical, but they gave me energy and were important to my ongoing happiness and productivity, so I ranked them as 'D' priorities as well.

Other roles such as author, speaker, and service through nonprofit boards and community activities were enjoyable but less critical in my life. These became my 'C' priorities. My 'B' priorities included important but less critical roles such as strategist, investor relations, sunday school teacher, and marketing director.

STEP 2:

❦

Prioritize your roles into A, B, and C categories.

7

TIME REQUIREMENT

Desires dictate our priorities, priorities shape our choices, and choices determine our actions.
                                                    —*Dallin H. Oaks*

We were now in our fifth week of meetings. Steve was pleased with my progress and so was I.

"I have really enjoyed this process, Steve. These exercises are really helping me to understand why I have had so many time management and relationship challenges in the past."

He smiled. "Well, our next exercise is going to make this even more obvious. This week, I need for you to take each of your roles and think about how much time it would take you to fully satisfy the role."

"What do you mean satisfy the role?" I asked.

"How much time will it take for you to satisfy yourself and others with your performance in the given role? For example, how many hours per week or month do you need to adequately serve your clients as their loan officer? How many hours per week do you need to adequately manage your employees? How many hours per week do you need to be a great husband and father? How many hours do you need to recharge through self-improvement and recreational activities?"

Steve continued. "The key here is that *both parties* must be satisfied by your performance within each role. If you want to be a great son, you must determine how many hours per week (or month) you need to see your parents, and how many hours they need to see you."

Wow, this was going to be tough. "So, I need to go through each role and allocate a certain number of hours per week or month for each one? That's not easy, Steve."

"It's not easy, but it is a critical part of this program. We must make sure you have enough time available to adequately complete your most important roles."

STEP 3:

∽◦∾

Determine how much time it will take to satisfy (meet both parties' expectations for) each of your roles.

8

PRUNING THE TREE

The most important thing in life is knowing the most important things in life.

—David F. Jakielo

I began analyzing each role's time requirement. I started with my most critical roles and worked my way down to those that were least critical.

I would think about and track how much time I needed to satisfy each of my roles. Some roles, such as loan officer or business developer, needed daily or weekly attention while other roles, such as nonprofit board positions, needed monthly (or less frequent) time and attention.

After hours of thought and analysis, I allocated a time requirement to every role. I added all of them up and came up with 147 hours per week. Unfortunately, I didn't have that many available hours. Each week consisted of 168 hours. If you sleep the recommended 7 hours per night, this only leaves you 119 hours!

Plus, I had certain limitations to my schedule. I tried to work out early in the morning and dropped my son off at school at 7:30 each morning. My goal was to be at work by 8:00 a.m.

I committed long ago that I would leave the office by 6:00 p.m. every evening and be home by 6:30 p.m. so that I could spend quality time with my wife and children. So, this meant I only had 50 hours available in my work week.

There were approximately three hours available in the evenings for family, self-improvement, and recreational time and, occasionally, community activities would eat into this time. Sometimes, I could squeeze in a few hours after the kids went to bed or on the weekends.

After adding evenings and weekends to my available time, I still only got to 100 hours. I certainly couldn't get to 147 hours.

I called Steve and was very frustrated. "Steve, it looks like I have more roles than hours."

He laughed, clearly expecting this issue to arise. "Yes, it does. Sean, it looks like you need to make some tough decisions. The time allocation step of our process is truly where the rubber meets the road. You must have adequate time to satisfy your most important roles."

One of the downsides of being a pleaser is that it's very hard to say no to people you care about. Consequently, I often commit to things I shouldn't commit to.

I looked at all of my time requirements and made a few minor adjustments, but it was obvious that if I was going to meet the time requirements of my most critical roles, I needed to reduce my commitments and learn to be more selective with my time.

I began to review my "C" level roles and responsibilities for possible time savings. It was very difficult because I had joined each organization for a particular reason, and I would disappoint certain people if I resigned.

I decided to limit my community involvement to no more than three organizations. This would reduce my time commitment and allow me to focus more heavily on these organizations and make a greater impact.

In the past, I also spent hours each week giving non-clients business advice. I loved this part of my job, but it had to be limited so that I could fulfill my more critical roles.

After hours of soul-searching and thought, I made some painful resignation calls to minimize my time commitments, and I instructed my assistant to minimize outside appointments.

I finally got my time commitments reduced to a number that would realistically fit into my schedule. I was almost ready to implement the new life management system!

STEP 4:

❧

Limit your roles so that you can satisfy the most important roles in the time you have available.

9

SETTING THE CALENDAR

"The mark of a great man is one who knows when to set aside
the important things in order to accomplish the vital ones."
—Brandon Sanderson

In our next weekly meeting, I gave Steve a full report on my progress. He knew how difficult it was to get to this point and he encouraged me to finish strong.

"I know this is a challenging process, Sean. Hang in there, we are almost finished!"

"I'm not giving up Steve. I see that this process can make a huge difference in my life. What's the next step?"

"Now, I want you to take your time requirements and actually place them on your calendar. For example, if you need eight hours per week for client service, it must show up somewhere on your calendar. It doesn't matter if it's one complete eight-hour day, four hours per day for two days, or two hours per day for four days, but it must actually have space on your calendar.

"Also, do your best to group similar tasks together so that you don't have to change mental gears too often throughout the day."

This made total sense to me. If I allocated time to each role and didn't set the time on my calendar, I would have no way of managing the process and time would continue to get away from me.

So, I took each role's time requirement and placed it on my calendar. I gave this a great deal of thought and tried to place similar tasks together on the same day so that I would be the most productive.

Every Monday was an employee management and leadership day. I would meet with key employees that day, prepare communications to the staff, review key reports, and organize everyone for the week.

Tuesday became my client management day. I would work on new loan requests, call past due accounts, touch base with key clients, and manage my accounts.

Wednesday was my investor relations day. I would focus on investor calls or visits to make sure my investors were satisfied with the performance of the bank and the level of information they were receiving.

Thursdays were sales and business development days. I would make sales calls and follow up with prospects I had been trying to recruit. I would also take a few outside meetings with businesses seeking advice on these days.

Fridays were project and cleanup days. I would catch up on reading, process accounts payable, review reports, and get organized during this day. I also set aside an hour to call friends or family on Fridays as well, and this brought me a great deal of enjoyment.

Evenings and weekends were allocated to family and personal roles, including writing my next book as well as much-needed recreation and down time so that I would stay fresh and avoid burnout. I would do my best not to work during these times.

Sometimes unexpected issues or interruptions would derail my well-planned day. While the goal is to minimize these occurrences, they are unavoidable. I would simply try to reallocate the time lost to another time on my calendar that had a lower priority. In reality, I found that these interruptions became rarer as I practiced the life management system because I was more proactive and organized.

Each day and time now had a specific focus and I tried very hard to not allow other activities to creep into this time. Things were definitely taking shape!

STEP 5:

∾

Place every role's time allocation on your calendar and avoid interruptions during this time.

10

ONE WEEK AT A TIME

What you get by achieving your goals is not as important as what you become by achieving your goals.
—Henry David Thoreau

A s I drove up the driveway for my last weekly meeting with Steve, I felt like a new person. I was more relaxed and focused. I wasn't trying to do fifteen different things at once anymore. Even better, I was early for our meeting!

Steve arrived, ready to go as usual. "Sean, you're almost there. This is the final meeting and you are off and running!"

"That is fantastic! What is the last step, Steve?"

"I want you to set a weekly goal for each role. Each week, you will think about each of your roles and determine the one thing you can do to make the greatest difference in that role."

I didn't quite understand what he was saying. "Can you give me an example?"

"Sure. Let's take your supervisor role. What is one thing you can do this week to improve your performance within this role??"

"I would like to have fifteen-minute sit-down meetings with all my direct reports each week. I can start that immediately."

"Perfect!" Steve said. "Now, each week I want you to set a goal for each of your roles. Can you see how powerful this process can be?"

"I sure can. Wow, I could really improve my effectiveness and performance with this process."

I sat a weekly goal for each and every one of my remaining roles. Sometimes they were simple, such as taking my family to dinner or turning my iPhone off at home. Other goals were much more challenging, like starting a fitness routine and eating healthier.

STEP 6:

❧

Set a weekly goal for each role.
What one thing can you do to improve your
performance within each role this week?

11

ACCOUNTABILITY

Discipline is the bridge between goals and accomplishment.
—*Jim Rohn*

Before our time together ended, Steve had one last tip for me.

"Sean, I would recommend that you find an accountability partner to share your weekly goals with. Your partner can hold you accountable for setting and meeting your goals so that you don't get busy and lose focus."

"That's a great idea. An accountability partner will help me stay consistent week after week." It took a couple of weeks, but I recruited a fantastic accountability partner. My partner was a close friend of mine who I could tell anything. We were at a similar stage of life and struggled with the same issues.

I sat my weekly role goals every Sunday evening and emailed them to my accountability partner. Then, I met with him every Friday afternoon to give an honest assessment of my week and whether or not I achieved my goals. He did the same with me.

Some weeks, I did great. Other weeks, I didn't do as well. When I did well, my partner encouraged and praised me.

When I missed the mark, he held me accountable and never let me off the hook. He is still my accountability partner today.

STEP 7:

❦

Find a trusted partner to hold you accountable for setting and achieving your weekly goals.

12

SATURDAYS WITH GRANDMA

The love of family and the admiration of friends are much more important than wealth and privilege.
—*Charles Kuralt*

I tweaked and adjusted Steve's strategies until they worked well for me. I named the process The Priority Promise Life Management System and began to share it with my friends. They loved it.

My life changed drastically after I implemented the system. Every hour of every day had a focus and a purpose.

I told my staff about the Priority Promise system, and explained that I would only be available for open door meetings during certain times. They understood and adapted well. Several of them implemented the program themselves. My assistant learned to be disciplined in scheduling and limiting my outside activities to four hours per week.

Emergencies and unexpected interruptions would occasionally pop up that caused me to stray from my calendar, but this was the exception rather than the rule. I would also need to make adjustments from time to time, as certain roles would need more time than others.

My life is certainly not perfect, but I feel like I have greater control of my life than ever before. I am more present and focused in all my interactions because I'm not constantly thinking about my lengthy to-do list. I make fewer mistakes because I'm not constantly multi-tasking. I invest in important relationships like never before, because I have time set aside on my calendar to call or email family and friends every week.

Best of all, I now spend wonderful Saturdays with Grandma Charlotte. On the first Saturday of every month, I take my kids down to Grandma and Grandpa's house at 10:00 a.m. We play, talk, and eat lunch together. She gets to know her great-grandchildren better and I get to know my grandparents better. I love Saturdays with Grandma.

13

THE BIG NEWS

"You need to make time for your family no matter what happens in your life."

— Matthew Quick,
The Silver Linings Playbook

About three months after I began to implement the Priority Promise System, I received a phone call from my mom.

"Sean, your Grandma Charlotte went to the doctor today and got some bad news. She has cancer. We don't know a lot yet, but this may not be good."

My heart dropped to the floor. I couldn't imagine our lives without Grandma Charlotte. She held our family together. She counseled us. She checked on us. She encouraged us. Holidays were always spent at her house. What would we do without her?

This time I immediately took the time to call Grandma Charlotte. Grandma had been diagnosed with lymphoma, which had a very wide range of possible outcomes. Some were manageable, but some were dire.

She was amazingly calm about the news. "Sean, God is in control. Your grandpa and I are going to continue to live our lives to the fullest and see how everything turns out. We don't want everyone to be sad and worried. If it's time for me to go to Heaven, then it's just my time. I have lived a wonderful life."

At that moment, it occurred to me that Grandma Charlotte and Grandpa Bill understood and practiced The Priority Promise at its best. They always had time for what was important.

My grandparents obviously loved each other and their family very much. When someone had a problem, they were there. They exercised regularly and took care of themselves. They were active in their church, took trips together, went out to dinner together on a regular basis, had good friends around them at all times, and generally enjoyed life.

Grandma and Grandpa always had time for us. They were never too busy to talk or listen. They weren't the wealthiest or most powerful family in town, but they were definitely one of the most beloved. They had been a tremendous example of how The Priority Promise can lead to a fulfilling and enjoyable life.

We are very early in the treatment process for Grandma Charlotte. She is starting chemotherapy and we are hopeful that the cancer can be contained. Only God knows how everything will turn out, but I do know that the Priority Promise has helped me prepare for this time. It has enabled me to take the time to focus on Grandma, help her look for the medical specialists she needs, and fully focus when we are together.

At the end of the day, nothing is more important than deep, rich relationships with those we love the most. I hope The Priority Promise system has the same impact on your life that it had on mine.

I am extremely grateful that this system has allowed me to spend more quality time with my grandmother.

Most importantly, I am grateful that I am no longer the invisible grandson.

AFTERWORD

Recently, I had an experience that further confirmed why life management is so important.

One of my best friends and clients shared an amazing experience with me that I want to share with you.

His granddaughter was born with a genetic defect and the doctors did not believe she would live, but she did. She grew into a gorgeous baby girl, always happy and full of life.

Unfortunately, the doctor's diagnosis proved true when, at the age of 18 months, she suddenly passed away. It was a heartbreaking experience for the family who had become so attached to her.

On the same day his granddaughter passed away, my client received the largest check in the history of his business. He had been working toward this moment for decades.

As he made a deposit into my bank that was beyond his wildest dreams, he didn't even care. All he could think about was his beautiful granddaughter.

So goes life. We spend our entire lives working for that big check, and it doesn't really matter. All that matters are relationships with the people we love.

My sincere hope is that you will allow the Priority Promise Life Management System to help you focus on the things that matter most in your life.

Priority Promise Resources

We have provided you with tools to implement the Priority Promise system on our website, www.theprioritypromise.net. These tools include:

1. Role forms: for entering and prioritizing your roles.

2. Role calendar: for allocating time to each role and placing it on your calendar.

3. Role goals: a form for entering your weekly role goals and recording your performance.

We all deserve to live a life of fulfillment and joy, and I hope that the Priority Promise system is your first step in making this a reality.

ABOUT THE AUTHOR

Sean Kouplen was a bank president, business owner, Chamber of Commerce president, his university's national alumni president, an award-winning professor, founder of a thriving nonprofit organization and community church, and Citizen of the Year in his hometown—all by the age of thirty-four.

Now at the age of thirty-nine, Kouplen's real passion is helping individuals live a fulfilling life by creating a clear vision for their future and developing and implementing a plan to achieve this vision.

Kouplen's first book, *Out of the Blocks* and its second addition, *12 Life Lessons Every Graduate Should Know*, helped college students effectively transition from the campus into the real world. It became a self-help bestseller, and Kouplen is a sought-after speaker for student and young professional groups throughout the nation.

Kouplen currently serves as President and CEO of Regent Bank in Tulsa, Oklahoma. He enjoys reading, playing golf, working on the family ranch with his father, and spending time with his wife Angela and their children, Emory, Kennedy, and Finley.

To learn more about the Priority Promise Life Management System and request Sean to speak to your group, please visit www.theprioritypromise.net.

CPSIA information can be obtained at www.ICGtesting.com
Printed in the USA
LVOW07*0328220515

439420LV00002B/27/P